The Making of Everyday Things

Sneakers

Derek Miller

New York

Published in 2020 by Cavendish Square Publishing, LLC
243 5th Avenue, Suite 136, New York, NY 10016

Copyright © 2020 by Cavendish Square Publishing, LLC

First Edition

No part of this publication may be reproduced, stored in a retrieval system, or transmitted in any form or by any means—electronic, mechanical, photocopying, recording, or otherwise—without the prior permission of the copyright owner. Request for permission should be addressed to Permissions, Cavendish Square Publishing, 243 5th Avenue, Suite 136, New York, NY 10016. Tel (877) 980-4450; fax (877) 980-4454.

Website: cavendishsq.com

This publication represents the opinions and views of the author based on his or her personal experience, knowledge, and research. The information in this book serves as a general guide only. The author and publisher have used their best efforts in preparing this book and disclaim liability rising directly or indirectly from the use and application of this book.

All websites were available and accurate when this book was sent to press.

Library of Congress Cataloging-in-Publication Data

Names: Miller, Derek L., author.
Title: Sneakers / Derek Miller.
Description: First edition. | New York : Cavendish Square, 2020. | Series: The making of everyday things | Includes bibliographical references and index.
Identifiers: LCCN 2018057079 (print) | LCCN 2018060631 (ebook) | ISBN 9781502646897 (ebook) | ISBN 9781502646880 (library bound) | ISBN 9781502646866 (pbk.) | ISBN 9781502646873 (6 pack)
Subjects: LCSH: Sneakers--Design and construction--Juvenile literature.
Classification: LCC TS1017 (ebook) | LCC TS1017 .M55 2020 (print) | DDC 685/.3102--dc23
LC record available at https://lccn.loc.gov/2018057079

Editorial Director: David McNamara
Copy Editor: Nathan Heidelberger
Associate Art Director: Alan Sliwinski
Designer: Ginny Kemmerer
Production Coordinator: Karol Szymczuk
Photo Research: J8 Media

The photographs in this book are used by permission and through the courtesy of: Cover Namning//Shutterstock.com;
p. 5 Tinna Pong/Shutterstock.com; p. 7 Indochina Studio/Shutterstock.com; p. 9 Photo Chaz/iStock/Getty Images; p. 11 MSPT/Shutterstock.com;
p. 13 Scott Eisen/Bloomberg/Getty Images; p. 15 Baona/iStock/Getty Images; p. 17 Jacobs Stock Photography/Photo Disc/Getty Images;
p. 19 Armmit/Shutterstock.com; p. 21 Monkey Business Images/Shutterstock.com.

Printed in the United States of America

Contents

Sneakers **4**

New Words **22**

Index **23**

About the Author............ **24**

Sneakers help us walk.

They help us run.

They help us play outside.

A sneaker has a **sole** and an **upper**.

The sole is the bottom.

The upper is the top.

The sole is made of rubber.

Rubber grips the ground.

It helps you to not slip.

The rubber sole is tough.

Sharp things can't get through.

The sole keeps your foot safe.

The upper is made from **fabric**.

The fabric is cut into pieces.

The pieces are **sewn** together.

Fabric is soft.

It is comfortable.

It keeps your feet warm.

The upper holds your foot in.

Laces are part of the upper.

Laces can be tied tight.

This makes sneakers fit.

The upper and the sole are put together.

Sometimes they are sewn.

Sometimes they are glued.

19

The sneakers are ready.

The parts work together.

They make sneakers fit.

Sneakers help us move!

New Words

fabric (FA-brik) Cloth.

sewn (SONE) Held together with thread.

sole (SOHL) The rubber bottom of a sneaker.

upper (UP-er) The top part of a sneaker.

Index

fabric, 12, 14

fit, 16, 20

glued, 18

laces, 16

rubber, 8, 10

safe, 10

sewn, 12, 18

sole, 6, 8, 10, 18

upper, 6, 12, 16, 18

warm, 14

About the Author

Derek Miller is a teacher and writer. He likes to learn interesting facts about things we see every day.

About

Bookworms help independent readers gain reading confidence through high-frequency words, simple sentences, and strong picture/text support. Each book explores a concept that helps children relate what they read to the world they live in.